DIVERSITY EQUALS US!

written by **Erica Cruz**

This book is dedicated to my lovely daughter, Evalisse Rodriguez.

AuthorHouse™
1663 Liberty Drive
Bloomington, IN 47403
www.authorhouse.com
Phone: 833-262-8899

Because of the dynamic nature of the Internet, any web addresses or links contained in this book may have changed since publication and may no longer be valid. The views expressed in this work are solely those of the author and do not necessarily reflect the views of the publisher, and the publisher hereby disclaims any responsibility for them.

This book is printed on acid-free paper.

ISBN: 978-1-6655-7063-3 (sc)
ISBN: 978-1-6655-7064-0 (e)

Library of Congress Control Number: 2022916949

Print information available on the last page.

Published by AuthorHouse 09/16/2022

authorHOUSE®

WELCOME, FRIENDS! I am about to

take you all on a cultural trip. So buckle up, and get ready to take off and learn about many different nationalities. Can we all prepare for departure? All right! Let's all count down from three and shout, "Take off!" Three, two, one, take off!

Hola, Mi nombre es Diego y soy de la Republica Domincana! [Hello, my name is Diego and I am from the Dominican Republic!] Welcome to Santo Domingo's Monumento a los Heroes de la Restauracion. This monument was built in 1953 and is located in the city of Santiago de los Caballeros in the Dominican Republic. It represents peace and honors the Dominican Republic's independence.

Hail up! My name is Avita. I am from Jamaica. Welcome to the Bob Marley Museum, located in Kingston, Jamaica. In 1985, Marley's wife converted the home into this museum to celebrate his life and legacy.

Como estás? Mi nombre es Luis y yo soy de Puerto Rico! [How are you? My name is Luis and I am from Puerto Rico!] Welcome to a famous landmark in Puerto Rico called El Castillo de San Felipe del Morro, which commenced in 1539 and finished in 1790. This refuge and its walls served as an active US military base during two world wars; the military also used it as an observation post. Did you know that Puerto Rico isn't a separate country? In fact, is a territory that is part of the United States.

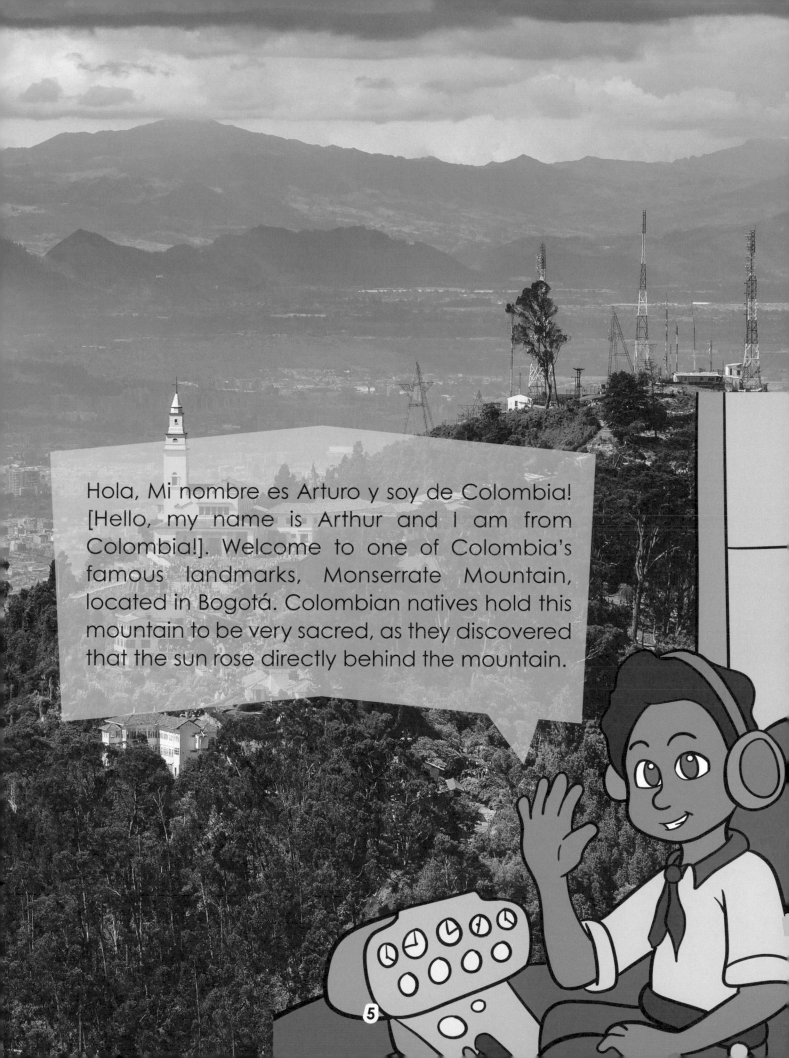

Hola, Mi nombre es Arturo y soy de Colombia! [Hello, my name is Arthur and I am from Colombia!]. Welcome to one of Colombia's famous landmarks, Monserrate Mountain, located in Bogotá. Colombian natives hold this mountain to be very sacred, as they discovered that the sun rose directly behind the mountain.

Namaste! My name is Aarush; I am from India. Welcome to the Taj Mahal Agra, a famous landmark in India located in the city of Agra. The emperor Shah Jahan built this structure between 1631 and 1648 to preserve the memory of his favorite wife.

Hello! My name is Emma. I am from the United States. Welcome to the Statue of Liberty, located on Liberty Island in New York Harbor. This statue was built in France between 1875 and 1884, then the French decided to gift it to the United States to represent commemoration of the alliance of France and the United States during the American Revolution. The statue was then shipped to New York City in 1885 and was reassembled on Liberty Island in 1886 to symbolize America's message of liberty to the world following the Declaration of Independence.

What is your name, and where are you from?

Conclusion: Welcome back and thank you all for flying with us on our cultural trip. I hope you all enjoyed your flight and the experiences of meeting some of our friends from different cultures. Well, it doesn't end here! There are still many more amazing countries around the world that we didn't get to visit. We hope to continue this journey of meeting more new friends and learning all about their amazing cultures as they learn about ours.

See you all soon!

Thinking outside the box activity:

How different do you think we are?

We are not actually very different. We may come from different backgrounds and traditions, and we may look different, have different personalities, speak different languages, eat different foods, and live in different parts of the world. All these differences make us unique but amazing.

But our amazing differences create diversity, and we should always embrace and be proud of where we come from and who we are. Although we may be unique, we are also the same because we are all humans! We all deserve the same equal respect, acknowledgment, and opportunities. Diversity is what brings unity, and unity is what provides us with love, empathy, harmony, and strength.

Just as our friends are diverse, so are our teachers, families, and communities as a whole.

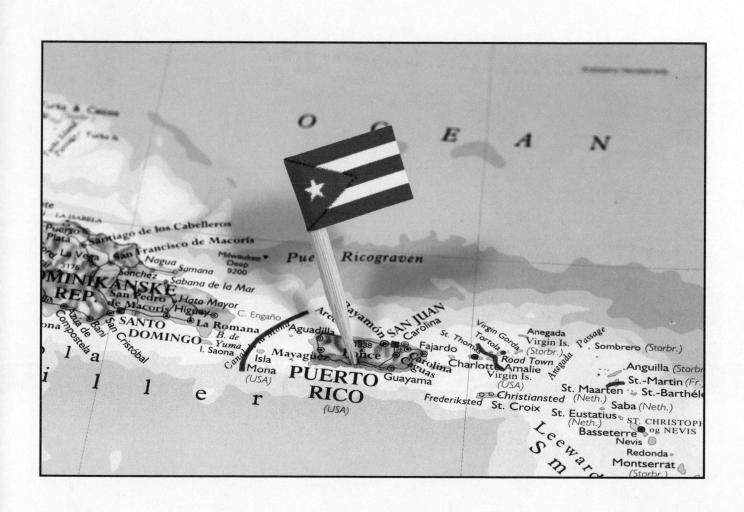

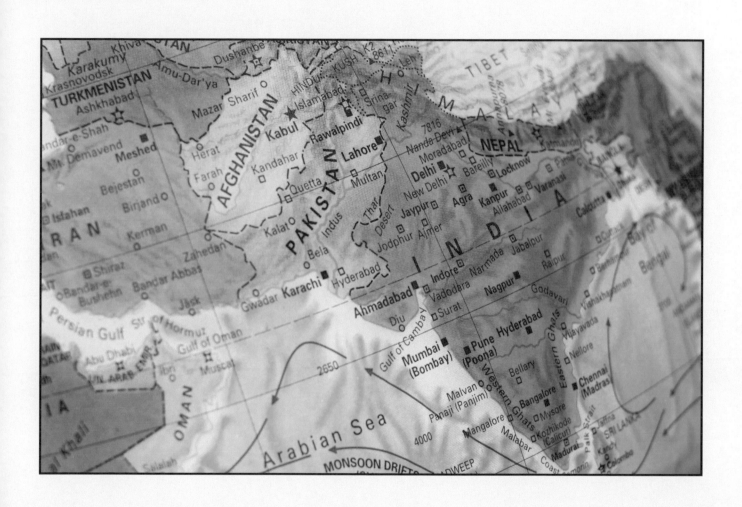

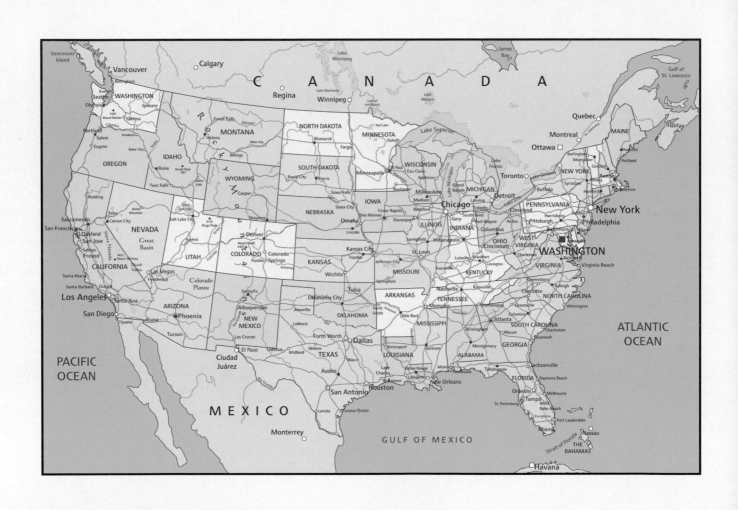

Printed in the United States
by Baker & Taylor Publisher Services